KETO DIE
COOKBOOK WITH
PICTURES

Healthy, Delicious and Simple Low-Carb,
High-Fat Recipes with The Best Ingredients.

Samuel Hayes

TABLE OF CONTENTS

Introduction

If your goals are to lose weight in a healthy way, prevent disease, and boost your general well-being, the ketogenic diet is the best option for you. Many people are adopting this low-carb, high-fat eating plan to enhance their health and shed extra pounds. Foods high in fat and protein and low in carbohydrates are the basis of the ketogenic diet. The ketogenic diet is tailor-made for you if you are a diabetic patient due to its remarkable efficacy in reversing the disease.

Most individuals nowadays eat a standard Western diet, which is abundant in carbohydrates and sugar.

This is why so many people have inflammatory problems and insulin resistance today. Unfortunately, their bodies have lost the ability to effectively burn excess fat, and the carbs they eat on a regular basis are impairing their livers' ability to do their job. You can control your blood sugar levels and restore your body's sensitivity to insulin with the help of the ketogenic diet. In just a few weeks, you can transform your body into a lean, fat-burning machine by sticking to the diet. Everyone knows that watching what you eat is crucial, but few actually do it. Nowadays, people are so rushed that they rarely stop to consider the nutritional value of the food they consume. These days, the majority of us eat a diet that's high in sugary and carbohydrate-rich meals. Insulin resistance and chronic inflammation are the results of a carb-based diet that many people follow on a regular basis.

Having a slim figure and losing weight are goals for most of us. However, the CDC reports that one-third of American adults are overweight or obese. The ketogenic diet is ideal for those who wish to reduce body fat while also decreasing their risk of developing serious illnesses such as cardiovascular disease, diabetes, and cancer. The ketogenic diet is a scientifically proven diet plan that restricts carbohydrate intake (such as that found in sugary foods, bread, and pasta) while increasing fat and protein consumption. The ketogenic diet is increasingly being recommended by dietitians and medical professionals due to its many health benefits. If you want to lose weight and get in shape without suffering any harmful side effects, this low-carb ketogenic diet book is for you. Use the advice in this book to eat well while decreasing your body fat.

Chapter 1 What Is the Ketogenic Diet?

The ketogenic diet is based on the theory that depriving the body of carbs, its main source of energy, will cause it to switch to using fat as fuel instead of carbohydrates, leading to rapid and dramatic weight loss. Carbohydrate-containing foods are broken down into glucose, often known as blood sugar, which the body needs for energy. Whenever possible, your body will first use glucose for energy before resorting to stored fat. The goal of the ketogenic diet is to reduce glucose levels and force the liver to metabolize fat for fuel instead of carbohydrates. Ketones are a byproduct of your metabolism that is produced when the liver breaks down fat. In the absence of glucose, the body can use these ketones as fuel.

How the diet works

If you take less than 50 grams of carbohydrates daily, your body will run out of readily available fuel or blood glucose. Usually, this will take about four days. The body will then begin to metabolize protein and fat for fuel, which may lead to weight loss.

What Is Ketosis?

The premise behind the ketogenic diet is that forcing the body into ketosis will increase the rate of fat loss. When glucose levels are depleted, the body enters a metabolic state known as ketosis to produce energy. When glycogen levels are low, the body switches to using fat for fuel. Ketones, an acid byproduct of this process, accumulate and can be used for energy.

The benefits of the Ketogenic Diet

Weight Loss

The keto diet is effective for weight loss because it forces the body to use stored fat for energy. During keto, your levels of insulin, the hormone that stores fat, drop by a lot. This turns your body into a fat-burning machine.

Control Blood Sugar

The ketogenic diet, due to the types of meals it encourages, has been shown to have a direct effect on lowering blood sugar. Compared to low-calorie diets, the ketogenic diet has been shown to be more beneficial in managing and preventing diabetes. A ketogenic diet is worth looking into if you are at risk for or already have Type II diabetes.

Mental Focus

The ketogenic diet is often used for its purported cognitive benefits. Brain cells thrive on ketones, which are a readily available fuel source. Reduced carbohydrate intake results in fewer and less severe fluctuations in blood sugar. When taken as a whole, this can help people concentrate better. Increased consumption of fatty acids has been shown to significantly improve cognitive performance.

Enhanced Stamina and Normalized Appetite

You will feel more energized throughout the day if you provide your body with a better and more consistent source of energy. Research indicates that fats are the most energy-dense molecules to burn. In addition, the satiating effects of fat last longer and reduce our hunger levels.

Cholesterol & Blood Pressure

Research shows that the risk factors for arterial plaque buildup—triglycerides and cholesterol—are reduced while on a ketogenic diet. In particular, when comparing low-fat and low-carbohydrate diets, the latter shows a considerable increase in HDL, while the former shows a drop in LDL particle concentration. It has been shown that blood pressure drops more on ketogenic diets than on any other type of diet.

Insulin Resistance

When unchecked, insulin resistance can progress to type II diabetes. There is a wealth of evidence demonstrating that a keto diet, which is low in carbohydrates, can help people with diabetes get their insulin levels back to normal.

What to eat and avoid?

Do Not Eat

- Grains –Rice, cereal, wheat, corn, etc.
- Sugar –Maple syrup, honey, agave, etc.
- Fruit –Oranges, apples, bananas, etc.

- Tubers –Yams, potatoes, etc.

Do Eat

- Meats – Eggs, poultry, fish, beef, lamb, etc.
- Leafy Greens – spinach, kale, etc.
- Above-ground vegetables – broccoli, cauliflower, etc.
- High Fat Dairy –high-fat cream, hard cheeses, butter, etc.
- Nuts and seeds –sunflower seeds, macadamias, walnuts, etc.
- Avocado and berries, blackberries, – raspberries, and other low glycemic impact berries
- Sweeteners –monk fruit, stevia, erythritol, and other low-carb sweeteners
- Other fats –high-fat salad dressing, coconut oil saturated fats, etc.

Chapter 2 Keto Problems and Solutions

Sustaining the ketogenic lifestyle: some advice

1. One of the main goals of the ketogenic diet is cutting out carbohydrates. Between 20 and 50 grams of carbs per day are optimal. Don't stress out over carb counting because it's simple.
2. On a ketogenic diet, you eat fewer carbs, but if you eat too much protein, it could raise your blood sugar.
3. Do not miss a single day of your diet. If you miss a day of your diet plan's schedule, you'll have to start over.
4. Fork it over numerous times before eating if you have any worries about the safety of the food or food item you are planning to eat.
5. For the first month of your diet, drink a cup of broth every day. The broth will aid in preventing the keto flu by keeping your electrolyte levels stable.
6. Before beginning your diet plan, it is a good idea to take images of your body from all angles. Then, evaluate the two after a month has passed. The loss of fat should motivate you to keep up with the ketogenic diet.
7. Learn all you can from newspaper columns, online publications, and blogs regarding the ketogenic diet. If you want to learn more about the keto diet, it's a good idea to read eBooks like this one and watch videos.
8. If you're feeling low, surround yourself with positive individuals. This individual could be your significant other or a close friend. If you can find an ally who believes in your cause, they will be a tremendous asset.
9. If you think you may benefit from vitamin or mineral supplementation, talk to your doctor.
10. Try new keto meals every week and play around with the ingredients. This will allow you to try many different dishes, increasing your enjoyment of the diet and helping you stick to it.
11. Get 8 glasses of water a day. Your desire for foods that are off-limits on the keto diet might be reduced by drinking water. Toxins and waste products can be flushed out of the body with the help of water.
12. Set a bedtime and attempt to wake up at the same time every day. Maintaining a regular sleeping schedule can assist you in controlling your food intake. Sleep deprivation has been shown to increase a person's appetite.
13. Instead of snacking on sweets like cookies and cupcakes, try munching on some fruits or veggies. You can satisfy your hunger in between meals by snacking on fruits, seeds, or nuts.

14. Eat 5 or 6 times a day, but avoid going too long without food, as this will cause you to overeat.

Some people on a diet have negative effects, such as

- Induction Flu: Symptoms include haziness of thought, irritation, fatigue, and sickness. During the first week of the diet, these symptoms are typical.

The cure: salt and water. The ingestion of sufficient water and salt will alleviate all of these signs and symptoms. You'd be wise to replace your usual beverage with broth.

- Leg Cramps: Leg cramps can become painful.

The cure: Achieve a healthy balance of salt and water in your diet. Magnesium supplements are also recommended. For the first three weeks, try taking three slow-release magnesium pills every day.

- Constipation: The diet also causes constipation.

The cure: The solution is simple: just drink more salty water. Eat a diet high in dietary fiber. Avoiding the need for laxatives altogether is another benefit of Milk of Magnesia.

- Bad Breath: Another unpleasant issue is bad breath.

The cure:

- Eat a bit more carb
- Get enough salt and drink enough fluid
- Maintain a good oral hygiene
- Heart palpitations

The cure: The simplest remedy is to simply drink enough water and take in enough fluids.

If you're still having trouble slimming down,

- Do not overdo it on the meat. If you eat a lot of protein, your body will turn that into glucose instead of entering ketosis.
- Stay away from sugar substitutes. All of these products, from cough syrup to chewing gum to mints, are loaded with sugar and artificial sweeteners.
- Avoid carb-heavy snacks, which contribute significantly to weight gain.

- You may be consuming too many foods high in carbohydrates. Incorporate some coconut oil into your diet and try to keep your carb intake to a minimum.
- Maybe you're consuming an excessive amount of fat in your diet. The diet is fat-based, but you're not allowed to overindulge.
- Stress and eating disorders are linked. The hormone cortisol is generated by the body in response to stress, and this hormone hinders weight loss efforts. Keep your cool under pressure.
- Excess fat storage is blocked by the hormone leptin. Leptin tells your brain when you've had enough to eat. Less leptin is sent to the brain as a person reduces their body fat percentage. Reduce leptin's influence by fueling your body with fat and protein.

Advice aimed at the ladies

- Women need to take a somewhat different approach to the ketogenic diet: Meats are notoriously difficult for our digestive systems to process. Eat more vegetables, broth, and sugar-free jello when your period is here.
- Eat plenty of fatty fish like sardines and salmon, organic beef, flaxseeds, and leafy greens to get your daily dose of omega-3 fats.
- Yogurt is beneficial to vaginal health since it includes "Lactobacillus acidophilus."
- If you want to keep your hormones in balance, mix almond milk with Vega, which is a whole-food smoothie with no added sugar, soy, or gluten.
- Losing weight can lead to sagging breasts, so it's important to work them out.
- Maintain a stable pH level. Incorporate lemon water into your daily routine.
- Periodic sugar cravings Eat low-carb chocolates.
- Try cranberry extract pills.

Chapter 3 Breakfast

KALE AVOCADO SMOOTHIE

Servings: 1
Prep Time: 5 minutes
Cook Time: None

Ingredients:

- 1 cup fresh chopped kale
- ½ cup chopped avocado
- ¾ cup unsweetened almond milk
- ¼ cup full-fat yogurt, plain
- 3 to 4 ice cubes
- 1 tablespoon fresh lemon juice
- Liquid stevia extract, to taste

Instructions:

1. Place the kale, avocado, and almond milk in a blender and pulse until well combined.
2. Give the items a few pulses in a food processor.
   Add in the other components and process until a smooth consistency is reached.
3. Pour into a large glass, and then consume it as soon as possible.

Nutrition Facts: 250 calories, 19g fat, 6g protein, 11.5g carbs

ALMOND BUTTER PROTEIN SMOOTHIE

Servings: 1
Prep Time: 5 minutes
Cook Time: None

Ingredients:

- 1 cup unsweetened almond milk
- ½ cup full-fat yogurt, plain
- ¼ cup vanilla egg white protein powder
- 1 tablespoon almond butter
- Pinch ground cinnamon
- Liquid stevia extract, to taste

Instructions:

1. Place the yogurt and almond milk in a blender and pulse until combined. Give the items a few pulses in a food processor. Add in the other components and process until a smooth consistency is reached.
2. Pour into a large glass, and then consume it as soon as possible.

Nutrition Facts: 315 calories, 16.5g fat, 31.5g protein, 12g carbs

BEETS AND BLUEBERRY SMOOTHIE

Servings: 1
Prep Time: 5 minutes
Cook Time: None

Ingredients:

- 1 cup unsweetened coconut milk
- ¼ cup heavy cream
- ¼ cup frozen blueberries
- 1 small beet, peeled and chopped
- 1 teaspoon chia seeds
- Liquid stevia extract, to taste

Instructions:

1. Put the blueberries, beets, and coconut milk into a blender and mix until smooth. Give the items a few pulses in a food processor.
2. Add in the other components and process until a smooth consistency is reached. Pour into a large glass, and then consume it as soon as possible.

Nutrition Facts: 215 calories, 17g fat, 2.5g protein, 15g carbs

ALMOND BUTTER MUFFINS

Servings: 12
Prep Time: 10 minutes
Cook Time: 25 minutes

Ingredients:

- 2 cups almond flour
- 1 cup powdered erythritol
- 2 teaspoons baking powder
- ¼ teaspoon salt
- ¾ cup almond butter, warmed
- ¾ cup unsweetened almond milk
- 3 large eggs

Instructions:

1. Place a muffin tin in the oven and preheat it to 350 degrees Fahrenheit while you line it with paper liners. In a mixing bowl, combine the almond flour, erythritol, baking powder, and salt by whisking all of the ingredients together.
2. In a separate bowl, combine the almond butter, almond milk, and eggs by whisking them together.
3. Combine the wet and dry ingredients. Mix until they are almost completely blended. Transfer the mixture by spoonfuls to the pan that has been prepared and bake for 22 to 25 minutes, or until a knife that has been inserted into the center comes out clean.
4. Allow the muffins to cool for about 5 minutes.

Nutrition Facts: 135 calories, 11g fat, 6g protein, 4g carbs

CLASSIC WESTERN OMELET

Servings: 1
Prep Time: 5 minutes
Cook Time: 10 minutes

Ingredients:

- 2 teaspoons coconut oil
- 3 large eggs, whisked
- 1 tablespoon heavy cream
- Salt and pepper
- ¼ cup diced green pepper
- ¼ cup diced yellow onion
- ¼ cup diced ham

Instructions:

1. In a separate bowl, whisk the eggs with the heavy cream, then season with salt and pepper.
   In a shallow skillet, melt 1 teaspoon of coconut oil over medium heat. After adding the peppers, onions, and ham, sauté everything for around three to four minutes.
2. Transfer the mixture to a bowl, then bring the skillet back up to temperature with the remaining oil.

After the eggs have been whisked, pour them into the pan and continue cooking until the bottom of the eggs begins to set.

Turn the skillet to evenly distribute the egg and continue to cook it until it is almost set.

3. After spreading the veggie and ham mixture over half of the omelet, fold the other half over the filling.

Wait for the eggs to reach the desired doneness before serving the omelet.

Nutrition Facts: 415 calories, 32.5g fat, 25g protein, 6.5g carbs

SHEET PAN EGGS WITH HAM AND PEPPER JACK

Servings: 6
Prep Time: 5 minutes
Cook Time: 15 minutes

Ingredients:

- 12 large eggs, whisked
- Salt and pepper
- 2 cups diced ham
- 1 cup shredded pepper jack cheese

Instructions:

1. Grease a baking sheet. Preheat the oven to 350 degrees Fahrenheit.
   In a bowl, beat the eggs with the salt and pepper until the mixture becomes foamy.
   Ham and cheese should be stirred together until they are thoroughly mixed.
2. Spread the mixture out in a uniform layer on the baking sheet after pouring the mixture there.
3. Bake the egg for 12 to 15 minutes until it has reached the desired consistency.
   After allowing it to somewhat cool, cut it into squares so that it can be served.

Nutrition Facts: 235 calories, 15g fat, 21g protein, 2.5g carbs

DETOXIFYING GREEN SMOOTHIE

Servings: 1
Prep Time: 5 minutes
Cook Time: None

Ingredients:

- 1 cup fresh chopped kale
- ½ cup fresh baby spinach
- ¼ cup sliced celery
- 1 cup water
- 4 ice cubes
- 2 tablespoons fresh lemon juice
- 1 tablespoon fresh lime juice
- 1 tablespoon coconut oil
- Liquid stevia extract, to taste

Instructions:

1. In a food processor, combine the kale, spinach, and celery. Repeat the process of pulsing the ingredients multiple times. Blend everything until it is completely smooth after adding the other components.
2. Pour into a large glass, and then consume it as soon as possible.

Nutrition Facts: 160 calories, 14g fat, 2.5g protein, 8g carbs

TOMATO MOZZARELLA EGG MUFFINS

Servings: 12
Prep Time: 5 minutes
Cook Time: 25 minutes

Ingredients:

- 1 tablespoon butter
- 1 medium tomato, finely diced
- ½ cup diced yellow onion
- 12 large eggs, whisked
- ½ cup canned coconut milk
- ¼ cup sliced green onion
- Salt and pepper
- 1 cup shredded mozzarella cheese

Instructions:

1. Spray a muffin pan with cooking spray. Turn the oven on to 350F. Butter should be melted in a skillet of medium size over medium heat.
2. After adding the tomato and onions, continue to cook for another three to four minutes until they have become softer.
3. Using a spoon, evenly distribute the mixture between the muffin cups.
4. After combining the eggs, coconut milk, green onions, salt, and pepper in a bowl with a whisk, transfer the mixture to muffin cups. After sprinkling with cheese, put the dish in the oven for 20 to 25 minutes.

Nutrition Facts: 135 calories, 10.5g fat, 9g protein, 2g carbs

BROCCOLI KALE EGG SCRAMBLE

Servings: 1
Prep Time: 5 minutes
Cook Time: 10 Minutes

Ingredients:

- 2 large eggs, whisked
- 1 tablespoon heavy cream
- Salt and pepper
- 1 teaspoon coconut oil
- 1 cup fresh chopped kale
- ¼ cup frozen broccoli florets, thawed
- 2 tablespoons grated parmesan cheese

Instructions:

1. In a bowl, use a whisk to combine the eggs with the heavy cream, then season with salt and pepper.
2. Warm up one teaspoon of coconut oil in a skillet that's medium-sized and set it over medium heat. After stirring in the kale and broccoli, continue cooking for about 1 to 2 minutes or until the kale has wilted.

3. Pour the eggs into the pan and continue to cook them, tossing them occasionally until they are almost set.
4. After stirring in the parmesan, the dish should be served hot.

Nutrition Facts: 315 calories, 23g fat, 19.5g protein, 10g carbs

THREE CHEESE EGG MUFFINS

Servings: 12
Prep Time: 5 minutes
Cook Time: 25 minutes

Ingredients:

- 1 tablespoon butter
- ½ cup diced yellow onion
- 12 large eggs, whisked
- ½ cup canned coconut milk
- ¼ cup sliced green onion
- Salt and pepper
- ½ cup shredded cheddar cheese
- ½ cup shredded Swiss cheese
- ¼ cup grated parmesan cheese

Instructions:

1. Spray a muffin pan with cooking spray. Turn the oven on to 350F.

2. Butter should be melted in a skillet of medium size over medium heat.
   After adding the onions, continue to simmer for another three to four minutes until they have become softer. Using a spoon, evenly distribute the mixture between the muffin cups.
3. After combining the eggs, coconut milk, green onions, salt, and pepper in a bowl with a whisk, transfer the mixture to muffin cups.
   In a bowl, mix all three cheeses together, then sprinkle them on top of the egg muffins.
4. Bake for approximately 20 to 25 minutes or until the egg has completely set.

Nutrition Facts: 150 calories, 11.5g fat, 10g protein, 2g carbs

STRAWBERRY RHUBARB PIE SMOOTHIE

Servings: 1
Prep Time: 5 minutes
Cook Time: None

Ingredients:

- 1 small stalk of rhubarb, sliced
- ¼ cup frozen sliced strawberries
- ¾ cup unsweetened cashew milk
- ½ cup full-fat yogurt, plain
- 1-ounce raw almonds
- ½ teaspoon vanilla extract
- Liquid stevia extract, to taste

Instructions:

1. Put the rhubarb, strawberries, and almond milk into a blender and mix until smooth. Repeat the process of pulsing the ingredients multiple times.
2. Blend everything until it is completely smooth after adding the other components.
3. Pour into a large glass, and then consume it as soon as possible.

Nutrition Facts: 285 calories, 20g fat, 11g protein, 17.5g carbs

CINNAMON ALMOND PORRIDGE

Servings: 1
Prep Time: 5 minutes
Cook Time: 5 minutes

Ingredients:

- 1 tablespoon butter
- 1 tablespoon coconut flour
- 1 large egg, whisked
- ⅛ teaspoon ground cinnamon
- Pinch salt
- ¼ cup canned coconut milk
- 1 tablespoon almond butter

Instructions:

1. In a small pot set over low heat, butter should be melted. Mix in the egg, cinnamon, and salt after whisking in the coconut flour.
2. While whisking, add the coconut milk and then stir in the almond butter until it is completely smooth. Keep the heat at a low simmer and stir the mixture often until it is completely hot.
3. Put everything in a bowl and serve.

Nutrition Facts: 470 calories, 42g fat, 13g protein, 15g carbs

BACON, MUSHROOM, AND SWISS OMELET

Servings: 1
Prep Time: 5 minutes
Cook Time: 10 minutes

Ingredients:

- 3 large eggs, whisked
- 1 tablespoon heavy cream
- Salt and pepper
- 2 slices uncooked bacon, chopped
- ¼ cup diced mushrooms
- ¼ cup shredded Swiss cheese

Instructions:

1. In a small bowl, combine the eggs, heavy cream, salt, and pepper by whisking them together. In a small skillet set over medium-high heat, cook the bacon until it is crispy.
2. After the bacon has reached the desired level of crispiness, place it in a bowl. After rewarming the skillet over medium heat, add the mushrooms to the pan.

29

3. After browning the mushrooms, remove them from the heat and place them in the bowl with the bacon. Reheat the skillet while adding the remaining oil to it. After the eggs have been whisked, pour them into the pan and continue cooking until the bottom of the eggs begins to set.
4. Turn the skillet to evenly distribute the egg and continue to cook it until it is almost set. On one half of the omelet, spread the mixture of bacon and mushrooms, then sprinkle with cheese and fold the other half over it. Wait for the eggs to reach the desired doneness before serving the omelet.

Nutrition Facts: 475 calories, 36g fat, 34g protein, 4g carbs

MAPLE CRANBERRY MUFFINS

Servings: 12
Prep Time: 10 minutes
Cook Time: 20 minutes

Ingredients:

- ¾ cups almond flour
- ¼ cup ground flaxseed
- ¼ cup powdered erythritol
- 1 teaspoon baking powder
- ⅛ teaspoon salt
- ⅓ cup canned coconut milk
- ¼ cup coconut oil, melted
- 3 large eggs
- ½ cup fresh cranberries
- 1 teaspoon maple extract

Instructions:

1. Set the oven to 350F. Line a muffin tin with paper cups.
   In a bowl, combine the ground flaxseed, erythritol, baking powder, and salt with the almond flour and whisk until well combined.
   In a separate bowl, combine the eggs, maple extract, coconut milk, and coconut oil by whisking them all together.
2. After mixing the dry and wet ingredients together until they are almost completely combined, fold in the cranberries.
3. Once you have spooned the batter into the prepared pan. Place it in the oven and bake for 18 to 20 minutes.
   After allowing the muffins to cool for 5 minutes in the pan, transfer them out onto a cooling rack made of wire.

Nutrition Facts: 125 calories, 11.5g fat, 3.5g protein, 3g carbs

Chapter 4 Lunch

BACON CHEESEBURGER SOUP

Servings: 4
Prep Time: 10 minutes
Cook Time: 15 minutes

Ingredients:

- slices of uncooked bacon
- 8 ounces ground beef (80% lean)
- 1 medium yellow onion, chopped
- 1 clove garlic, minced
- 3 cups beef broth
- 2 tablespoons tomato paste
- 2 teaspoons Dijon mustard
- Salt and pepper
- 1 cup shredded lettuce
- ½ cup shredded cheddar cheese

Instructions:

1   The bacon should be cooked in a saucepan until it becomes crispy, after which it should be drained on paper towels and chopped. In a saucepan, reheat the grease rendered from the bacon, then add the meat. After the beef has reached the desired color, remove half of the fat from the pan and continue cooking.

2   Bring the saucepan back up to temperature, then add the onion and garlic and continue cooking for another 6 minutes. After stirring in the stock, tomato paste, and mustard, season the mixture with salt and pepper to taste. After adding the beef, reduce the heat to medium-low, cover, and simmer for 15 minutes.

3   Place a heaping spoonful in each bowl and top with crumbled lettuce, grated cheddar cheese, and crumbled bacon.

Nutrition Facts: 315 calories, 20g fat, 27g protein, 6g carbs

BACON, LETTUCE, TOMATO, AVOCADO SANDWICH

Servings: 1
Prep Time: 30 minutes
Cook Time: None

Ingredients:

- 1 large egg, separated
- Pinch cream of tartar
- Pinch salt
- 1-ounce cream cheese softened
- 2 slices uncooked bacon
- ¼ cup sliced avocado
- ¼ cup shredded lettuce
- 1 slice tomato

Instructions:

1. In order to prepare the bread, bring an oven to a temperature of 300F. Line a baking sheet with parchment paper.

2. Cream of tartar, egg whites, and a pinch of salt should be beaten together until soft peaks form.
3. Cream cheese and egg yolk should be whisked together until the mixture is smooth and a pale-yellow color.
4. Egg whites should be folded in a bit at a time until the mixture is smooth.
   Using a spoon, spread the batter into two even circles on the baking sheet.
   Bake for 25 minutes until the center is solid and the edges have a light golden color.
5. After cooking the bacon in a pan until it's nice and crisp, put it on a paper towel to drain.
   Put together the sandwich using the bacon, avocado, lettuce, and tomato as the individual components.

Nutrition Facts: 355 calories, 30g fat, 16.5g protein, 5.5g carbs

FRIED SALMON CAKES

Servings: 2
Prep Time: 15 minutes
Cook Time: 10 minutes

Ingredients:

- 1 tablespoon butter
- 1 cup riced cauliflower
- Salt and pepper
- 8 ounces boneless salmon fillet
- ¼ cup almond flour
- 2 tablespoons coconut flour
- 1 large egg
- 2 tablespoons minced red onion
- 1 tablespoon fresh chopped parsley
- 2 tablespoons coconut oil

Instructions:

1. In a skillet, melt the butter. Once the butter is melted, sauté the cauliflower for five minutes or until it reaches the desired tenderness. Season with salt and pepper. Place the cauliflower in a bowl and bring the skillet back up to temperature.
2. After adding the salmon, season it with pepper and salt. Once the salmon has reached the desired doneness, remove it from the heat and flake it onto a bowl. To the bowl with the almond flour, coconut flour, egg, red onion, and parsley, add the cauliflower and stir to combine.
3. Form into six patties, then cook in coconut oil until brown on both sides of each patty.

Nutrition Facts: 505 calories, 37.5g fat, 31g protein, 14.5g carbs

SESAME CHICKEN AVOCADO SALAD

Servings: 2
Prep Time: 10 minutes
Cook Time: None

Ingredients:

- 1 tablespoon sesame oil
- 8 ounces of boneless chicken thighs, chopped
- Salt and pepper
- cups fresh spring greens
- 1 cup sliced avocado
- 2 tablespoons olive oil
- 2 tablespoons rice wine vinegar
- 1 tablespoon sesame seeds

Instructions:

1 In a skillet, bring the oil from the sesame seeds to a medium-high temperature.
2 The chicken should be seasoned with salt and pepper before being added to the skillet. While the chicken is cooking, stir it frequently and cook it until it is browned all the way through.

3   Take the chicken away from the fire and let it cool down a little bit. To make the salad, divide the spring greens between two dishes and top each with avocado. Olive oil and rice vinegar should be drizzled over the salads before serving.

4   When ready to serve, top with cooked chicken and sprinkle with toasted sesame seeds.

Nutrition Facts: 540 calories, 47.5g fat, 23g protein, 10.5g carbs

SPINACH CAULIFLOWER SOUP

Servings: 4
Prep Time: 5 minutes
Cook Time: 15 minutes

Ingredients:

- 1 tablespoon coconut oil
- 1 small yellow onion, chopped
- 2 cloves garlic, minced
- 2 cups chopped cauliflower
- 8 ounces fresh baby spinach, chopped
- cups vegetable broth
- ½ cup canned coconut milk
- Salt and pepper

Instructions:

1   In a saucepan, warm the oil over medium-high heat and add the onion and garlic at
    the same time. After browning for around four to five minutes in the sauté pan, mix

in the cauliflower. After browning the meat for five minutes, toss in the spinach and continue cooking.

2   It should be cooked for two minutes until it has wilted, after which the broth should be stirred in and brought to a boil. Take the soup off the heat and, using an immersion blender, make a smooth puree.

3   Mix in the coconut milk, then taste and adjust the seasoning with salt and pepper as desired. To be served hot.

Nutrition Facts: 165 calories, 12g fat, 7g protein, 9g carbs

CHEESY BUFFALO CHICKEN SANDWICH

Servings: 1
Prep Time: 30 minutes
Cook Time: None

Ingredients:

- 1 large egg, separated into white and yolk
- Pinch cream of tartar
- Pinch salt
- 1-ounce cream cheese softened
- 1 cup cooked chicken breast, shredded
- 2 tablespoons hot sauce
- 1 slice Swiss cheese

Instructions:

1   In order to prepare the bread, bring an oven to a temperature of 300F. Line a baking sheet with parchment paper. Cream of tartar, Egg whites, and a pinch of salt should be beaten together until soft peaks form. Cream cheese and egg yolk should be whisked together until the mixture is smooth and a pale-yellow color

2 Egg whites should be folded in a bit at a time until the mixture is smooth. Using a spoon, spread the batter into two even circles on the baking sheet. Bake for 25 minutes until the center is solid and the edges have a light golden color.

3 Shred the chicken and placed it in a basin. Then pour the hot sauce over the chicken. Place some of the chicken in the center of one of the bread circles, and then sprinkle some cheese on top. Place the other bread circle on top, and then dig in!

Nutrition Facts: 555 calories, 33.5g fat, 58g protein, 3.5g carbs

COCONUT CHICKEN TENDERS

Servings: 4
Prep Time: 10 minutes
Cook Time: 30 minutes

Ingredients:

- ¼ cup almond flour
- 2 tablespoons shredded unsweetened coconut
- ½ teaspoon garlic powder
- 2 pounds of boneless chicken tenders
- Salt and pepper
- 2 large eggs, whisked well

Instructions:

1   Turn the oven temperature up to 400F. Line a baking sheet with parchment paper. On a shallow plate, mix the almond flour, coconut, and garlic powder together until well combined.

2   After seasoning the chicken with salt and pepper, it should be dipped in the eggs that have been beaten.
3   Before putting the chicken tenders on the baking sheet, they should be dredged in the almond flour mixture. Bake for about 25 to 30 minutes, until the outside is browned and the inside is fully cooked. To be served hot.

Nutrition Facts: 325 calories, 9.5g fat, 56.5g protein, 2g carbs

CAULIFLOWER LEEK Soup WITH PANCETTA

Servings: 4
Prep Time: 15 minutes
Cook Time: 1 hour

Ingredients:

- cups chicken broth
- ½ medium head cauliflower, chopped
- 1 cup sliced leeks
- ½ cup heavy cream
- Salt and pepper
- 2 ounces diced pancetta

Instructions:

1   Mix the cauliflower and broth together in a saucepan and place it over medium-high heat.
2   The sliced leeks should be added after the chicken stock has been brought to a boil. Cauliflower should be cooked over medium heat with the lid on for one hour or until it is soft. Take the soup off the heat and, using an immersion blender, make a smooth puree.

3   After stirring in the cream, season with salt and pepper to taste. Cook the pancetta that has been diced in a skillet set over medium-high heat until it becomes crispy. When ready to serve, ladle the soup into bowls and top each one with pancetta.

Nutrition Facts: 200 calories, 13g fat, 12g protein, 8.5g carbs

THREE MEAT AND CHEESE SANDWICH

Servings: 1
Prep Time: 30 minutes
Cook Time: 5 minutes

Ingredients:

- 1 large egg, separated
- Pinch cream of tartar
- Pinch salt
- 1-ounce cream cheese softened
- 1-ounce sliced ham
- 1 ounce sliced hard salami
- 1-ounce sliced turkey
- 2 slices cheddar cheese

Instructions:

1   In order to prepare the bread, bring an oven to a temperature of 300F. Line a baking sheet with parchment paper.

2   Cream of tartar, Egg whites, and a pinch of salt should be beaten together until soft peaks form. Cream cheese and egg yolk should be whisked together until the mixture is smooth and a pale yellow color.
3   Egg whites should be folded in a bit at a time until the mixture is smooth.
4   Using a spoon, spread the batter into two even circles on the baking sheet.
    Bake for 25 minutes until the center is solid and the edges have a light golden color.
5   After you have layered the cut meats and cheeses between the two bread circles, the sandwich should be complete.
    Spray a skillet with cooking spray and place it in a medium-heated oven.
    After adding the sandwich, fry it until the underside is browned, then flip it and continue cooking until the cheese is almost completely melted.

Nutrition Facts: 610 calories, 48g fat, 40g protein, 3g carbs

BEEF AND PEPPER KEBABS

Servings: 2
Prep Time: 30 minutes
Cook Time: 10 minutes

Ingredients:

- 2 tablespoons olive oil
- 1 ½ tablespoons balsamic vinegar
- teaspoons Dijon mustard
- Salt and pepper
- 8 ounces beef sirloin, cut into 2-inch pieces
- 1 small red pepper, cut into chunks
- 1 small green pepper, cut into chunks

Instructions:

1   In a shallow dish, combine the olive oil, balsamic vinegar, and mustard by whisking them together.

2   After adding salt and pepper, toss the steak in the marinade. Marinate for at least an hour. After letting the meat sit in the marinade for half an hour, alternate the meat and peppers on skewers.

3   Prepare a grill pan by heating it over high heat and spraying it with cooking spray before using it. Cook the kebabs for two to three minutes per side or until the beef is no longer pink in the center.

Nutrition Facts: 365 calories, 21.5g fat, 35.5g protein, 6.5g carbs

SIMPLE TUNA SALAD ON LETTUCE

Servings: 2
Prep Time: 10 minutes
Cook Time: None

Ingredients:

- ¼ cup mayonnaise
- 1 tablespoon fresh lemon juice
- 1 tablespoon pickle relish
- 2 (6-ounce) cans tuna in oil, drained and flaked
- ½ cup cherry tomatoes halved
- ¼ cup diced cucumber
- Salt and pepper
- 2 cups chopped romaine lettuce

Instructions:

1   In a bowl, combine the mayonnaise, lemon juice, and relish by whisking them together.

2   Mix in the tuna flakes, tomatoes, and cucumbers, and then season with salt and pepper. To serve, drizzle the dressing over the chopped lettuce.

Nutrition Facts: 550 calories, 35g fat, 48g protein, 8.5g carbs

HAM, EGG, AND CHEESE SANDWICH

Servings: 1
Prep Time: 30 minutes
Cook Time: 5 minutes

Ingredients:

- 1 large egg, separated
- Pinch cream of tartar
- Pinch salt
- 1-ounce cream cheese softened
- 1 large egg
- 1 teaspoon butter
- ounces sliced ham
- 1 slice of cheddar cheese

Instructions:

1   In order to prepare the bread, bring an oven to a temperature of 300F. Line a baking sheet with parchment paper.
Cream of tartar, Egg whites, and a pinch of salt should be beaten together until soft peaks form.

2   Cream cheese and egg yolk should be whisked together until the mixture is smooth and a pale yellow color.
3   Egg whites should be folded in a bit at a time until the mixture is smooth.
4   Using a spoon, spread the batter into two even circles on the baking sheet.
    Bake for 25 minutes until the center is solid and the edges have a light golden color.
5   Fry the egg in butter until it is cooked to your liking, then add it to the sandwich to finish it off.
6   Place the ham slices in an attractive pattern on top of one of the bread circles.
    On top of the first bread circle, place the sliced cheese, then the fried egg, and finish with the second bread circle.
7   You can serve it immediately, or you can first melt the cheese in a skillet that has been buttered.

Nutrition Facts: 530 calories, 40g fat, 36g protein, 5.5g carbs

BACON-WRAPPED HOT DOGS

Servings: 2
Prep Time: 10 minutes
Cook Time: 30 minutes

Ingredients:

- all-beef hot dogs
- 2 slices cheddar cheese
- slices of uncooked bacon

Instructions:

1   Cut the hotdogs in half lengthwise, then make a cut halfway through the thickness of each one. To pack the cheese slices into the hot dogs, cut each slice in half lengthwise and use one half for each dog.
2   After wrapping the hotdogs in bacon, place them in a roasting pan that has been coated with foil. Bake the bacon for 30 minutes or until it reaches the desired level of crispiness.

Nutrition Facts: 500 calories, 43g fat, 24g protein, 4g carbs

Chapter 5 Dinner

GRILLED PESTO SALMON WITH ASPARAGUS

Servings: 4
Prep Time: 5 minutes
Cook Time: 15 minutes

Ingredients:

- (6-ounce) boneless salmon fillets
- Salt and pepper
- 1 bunch of asparagus, ends trimmed
- tablespoons olive oil
- ¼ cup basil pesto

Instructions:

1   Oil the grate of a grill before preheating it to a high temperature.
    After seasoning the salmon with salt and pepper, spray it with cooking spray and set it aside.
2   Cook the salmon on the grill for about 5 minutes per side or until it is fully done.
3   Oil the spears of asparagus, then grill them for about ten minutes.
    The salmon should be topped with pesto, and it should be served with asparagus.

Nutrition Facts: 300 calories, 17.5g fat, 34.5g protein, 2.5g carbs

SESAME-CRUSTED TUNA WITH GREEN BEANS

Servings: 4
Prep Time: 15 minutes
Cook Time: 5 minutes

Ingredients:

- ¼ cup white sesame seeds
- ¼ cup black sesame seeds
- (6-ounce) ahi tuna steaks
- Salt and pepper
- 1 tablespoon olive oil
- 1 tablespoon coconut oil
- cups green beans

Instructions:

1. Mix the two different kinds of sesame seeds together in a wide-mouthed bowl. Add some salt and pepper to the tuna and set it aside.
2. Run the tuna through the sesame seed mixture to coat it.

3   After bringing the olive oil to a high temperature in a skillet, add the tuna to the pan.

4   Turn the meat over and sear it on the second side after it has been seared on the first side for one to two minutes. Take the tuna out of the skillet and allow it to rest while you bring the skillet back up to temperature with the coconut oil.

5   Fry the green beans for about five minutes in the oil, and then serve them with sliced tuna.

Nutrition Facts: 380 calories, 19g fat, 44.5g protein, 8g carbs

ROSEMARY ROASTED PORK WITH CAULIFLOWER

Servings: 4
Prep Time: 10 minutes
Cook Time: 20 minutes

Ingredients:

- 1 ½ pounds boneless pork tenderloin
- 1 tablespoon coconut oil
- 1 tablespoon fresh chopped rosemary
- Salt and pepper
- 1 tablespoon olive oil
- cups cauliflower florets

Instructions:

1 Coconut oil should be used to coat the pork, and then rosemary, salt, and pepper should be added as seasonings.
2 To preheat the olive oil, place it in a big skillet and set it over medium-high heat. After adding the pork, sauté it for about three minutes on each side or until it has a browned appearance.

3   The pork should be surrounded by cauliflower that has been sprinkled in the pan. After turning the heat down to a low setting, cover the skillet and continue to cook the pork for another 8 to 10 minutes until it is fully done.
4   The pork should be served sliced alongside the cauliflower.

Nutrition Facts: 300 calories, 15.5g fat, 37g protein, 3g carbs

BEEF AND BROCCOLI STIR-FRY

Servings: 4
Prep Time: 20 minutes
Cook Time: 15 minutes

Ingredients:

- ¼ cup soy sauce
- 1 tablespoon sesame oil
- 1 teaspoon garlic chili paste
- 1 pound beef sirloin
- tablespoons almond flour
- tablespoons coconut oil
- 2 cups chopped broccoli florets
- 1 tablespoon grated ginger
- cloves garlic, minced

Instructions:

1 In a small bowl, combine the chili paste, sesame oil, and soy sauce by whisking them together. After slicing the meat, sprinkle it with the almond flour and place it in a plastic bag for the freezer.
2 After pouring in the sauce, give everything a quick toss to coat it, then set it aside for 20 minutes.
3 Bring the oil to a boil in a large skillet over medium-high heat. After pouring the steak and sauce into the skillet, begin to cook the beef until it has a browned appearance. When you're ready to cook the broccoli, ginger, and garlic, push the beef to the sides of the skillet. Sauté the broccoli until it is crisp-tender, then mix everything together and serve it hot.

Nutrition Facts: 350 calories, 19g fat, 37.5g protein, 6.5g carbs

HEARTY BEEF AND BACON CASSEROLE

Servings: 8
Prep Time: 25 minutes
Cook Time: 30 minutes

Ingredients:

- slices of uncooked bacon
- 1 medium head cauliflower, chopped
- ¼ cup canned coconut milk
- Salt and pepper
- pounds of ground beef (80% lean)
- ounces mushrooms, sliced
- 1 large yellow onion, chopped
- cloves garlic, minced

Instructions:

1   Turn the oven temperature up to 375 degrees F. The bacon should be cooked in a
    skillet until it is crispy, after which it should be drained on paper towels and chopped.

The cauliflower should be added to salted water that has been brought to a boil in a pot.

2 After boiling for 6 to 8 minutes, until the vegetables are soft, strain them and place them in a food processor together with the coconut milk. After blending the ingredients until they are completely smooth, season them with salt and pepper.

3 After browning the beef in a skillet, remove the fat from the steak before serving. After stirring in the mushrooms, onion, and garlic, pour the mixture into an oven-safe dish. Spread the cauliflower mixture over the top, then put it in the oven for half an hour.

4 minutes under the broiler at high heat, and then serve with bacon crumbles sprinkled on top.

Nutrition Facts: 410 calories, 25.5g fat, 37g protein, 7.5g carbs

FRIED COCONUT SHRIMP WITH ASPARAGUS

Servings: 6
Prep Time: 15 minutes
Cook Time: 10 minutes

Ingredients:

- 1 ½ cups shredded unsweetened coconut
- large eggs
- Salt and pepper
- 1 ½ pounds large shrimp, peeled and deveined
- ½ cup canned coconut milk
- 1 pound asparagus, cut into 2-inch pieces

Instructions:

1   Place the coconut in a bowl with a shallow profile. In a bowl, whisk the eggs while adding some pepper and salt to taste. After the shrimp have been dipped in the egg, dredge them in the coconut.
2   In a large skillet, bring the coconut oil to a warm temperature.

3   After adding the shrimp, cook them for one to two minutes per side until they are golden. Take the shrimp out of the pan and place them on some paper towels.
4   Then, reheat the skillet. After adding the asparagus and seasoning it with salt and pepper, sauté it for a few minutes until it is crisp-tender, and then serve it alongside the shrimp.

Nutrition Facts: 535 calories, 38.5g fat, 29.5g protein, 18g carbs

COCONUT CHICKEN CURRY WITH CAULIFLOWER RICE

Servings: 6
Prep Time: 15 minutes
Cook Time: 30 minutes

Ingredients:

- 1 tablespoon olive oil
- 1 medium yellow onion, chopped
- 1 ½ pounds boneless chicken thighs, chopped
- Salt and pepper
- 1 (14-ounce) can of coconut milk
- 1 tablespoon curry powder
- 1 ¼ teaspoon ground turmeric
- cups riced cauliflower

Instructions:

1   Bring the oil to a medium temperature in a large skillet. After about 5 minutes of cooking, add the onions and continue to cook until they are transparent.

2   After giving it a good toss and seasoning it with salt and pepper, add the chicken and cook it for six to eight minutes, stirring it frequently, until it is browned on both sides.
3   After adding the curry powder and turmeric to the skillet with the coconut milk, give everything a good swirl. Keep the mixture at a low simmer for 15–20 minutes or until it is hot and bubbling.
4   While this is going on, steam the cauliflower rice with a few tablespoons of water until it reaches the desired consistency. The cauliflower rice should be served atop the curry.

Nutrition Facts: 430 calories, 29g fat, 33.5g protein, 9g carbs

SPICY CHICKEN ENCHILADA CASSEROLE

Servings: 6
Prep Time: 15 minutes
Cook Time: 1 hour

Ingredients:

- pounds boneless chicken thighs, chopped
- Salt and pepper
- cups tomato salsa
- 1 ½ cups shredded cheddar cheese
- ¾ cup sour cream
- 1 cup diced avocado

Instructions:

1   Grease a casserole dish and heat the oven to 375 degrees Fahrenheit before putting it in. First, the chicken is seasoned with salt and pepper, and then it is distributed around the dish.

2   After spreading the salsa over the chicken, top it with the grated cheese. Wrap the chicken in foil, then place it in the oven for one hour or until it reaches the desired doneness.

3   Serve with sour cream and avocado that have been chopped.

Nutrition Facts: 550 calories, 31.5g fat, 54g protein, 12g carbs

CHEDDAR, SAUSAGE, AND MUSHROOM CASSEROLE

Servings: 6
Prep Time: 15 minutes
Cook Time: 35 minutes

Ingredients:

- 1 pound ground Italian sausage
- ounces mushrooms, diced
- 1 large yellow onion, chopped
- 1 cup shredded cheddar cheese
- large eggs
- ½ cup heavy cream
- Salt and pepper

Instructions:

1 Prepare a baking dish by greasing it and setting the oven to 375 degrees Fahrenheit. In a large skillet, bring the sausage to an appropriate temperature.
2 Brown, the sausage, add the mushrooms and onions and mix to combine.

3   After cooking for four to five minutes, spread the mixture evenly in the baking dish. After sprinkling the dish with cheese, mix the rest of the ingredients in another bowl with a whisk.

4   After pouring the mixture into the dish, place it in the oven for 35 minutes or until the mixture is bubbling.

Nutrition Facts: 450 calories, 34g fat, 28g protein, 6g carbs

CAULIFLOWER CRUST MEAT LOVER'S PIZZA

Servings: 2
Prep Time: 20 minutes
Cook Time: 20 minutes

Ingredients:

- 1 tablespoon butter
- cups riced cauliflower
- Salt and pepper
- 1 ½ cups shredded mozzarella cheese, divided into 1 cup and ½ cup
- 1 cup fresh grated parmesan
- 1 teaspoon garlic powder
- 1 large egg white
- 1 teaspoon dried Italian seasoning
- ¼ cup low-carb tomato sauce
- ounces sliced pepperoni
- 1-ounce diced ham
- 2 slices bacon, cooked and crumbled

Instructions:

1 Turn the oven temperature up to 400F. Line a baking sheet with parchment paper. Stir the cauliflower into the melted butter that has been heated in a skillet over medium-high heat.

2 After seasoning with salt and pepper, cover the pot and place it over medium heat. Check the vegetables for doneness after 15 minutes by stirring them occasionally. Put the cauliflower in a bowl and toss in the mozzarella, parmesan, and garlic powder. If you like, sprinkle some garlic powder on top. After stirring in the egg white and Italian spice, pour the batter onto the baking sheet that has been prepared.

3 After shaping the dough into a circle with a thickness of around 12 inches, bake it for 15 minutes.

4 The remaining mozzarella, pepperoni, bacon, and ham are layered on top of the tomato sauce, which is then topped with the tomato sauce.
Wait until the cheese has a browned appearance under the broiler, then slice it to serve.

Nutrition Facts: 560 calories, 40.5g fat, 41g protein, 11g carbs

PEPPER GRILLED RIBEYE WITH ASPARAGUS

Servings: 4
Prep Time: 5 minutes
Cook Time: 15 minutes

Ingredients:

- 1 pound asparagus, trimmed
- tablespoons olive oil
- Salt and pepper
- 1 pound ribeye steak
- 1 tablespoon coconut oil

Instructions:

1 Set the oven to 400F and cover a small baking sheet with aluminum foil. Olive oil should be used to coat the asparagus, and then it should be spread out on a baking pan.
2 After you have seasoned it with salt and pepper, put it in the oven. Sprinkle some pepper and salt on the meat, then rub it with pepper.
3 In a skillet made of cast iron, melt the coconut oil while the skillet is heated to a high temperature.

4   After adding the steak, heat it for two minutes without turning it, then flip it. Put the skillet in the oven and keep cooking the steak for another 5 minutes or until it's done to your liking.

5   After roasting the asparagus, slice the steak and serve it with the asparagus.

Nutrition Facts: 380 calories, 25g fat, 35g protein, 4.5g carbs

BACON-WRAPPED PORK TENDERLOIN WITH CAULIFLOWER

Servings: 4
Prep Time: 10 minutes
Cook Time: 25 minutes

Ingredients:

- 1 ¼ pounds boneless pork tenderloin
- Salt and pepper
- slices of uncooked bacon
- 1 tablespoon olive oil
- cups cauliflower florets

Instructions:

1 Before serving, season the pork with salt and pepper and heat the oven to 425 degrees Fahrenheit. Wrap the pork with bacon and set it in a roasting pan that has been coated with foil.
2 Roast for another 25 minutes or until an internal temperature of 155 degrees Fahrenheit is reached. In the meantime, bring the oil to temperature in a skillet set over medium heat. After adding the cauliflower, sauté it for about 8 to 10 minutes or until it is crisp-tender.

3   Preheat the broiler and place the pig on the middle rack of the oven to brown the bacon. Cut the pork into slices and serve it with the cauliflower that has been sautéed.

Nutrition Facts: 330 calories, 18.5g fat, 38g protein, 3g carbs

STEAK KEBABS WITH PEPPERS AND ONIONS

Servings: 4
Prep Time: 30 minutes
Cook Time: 10 minutes

Ingredients:

- 1 pound beef sirloin, cut into 1-inch cubes
- ¼ cup olive oil
- tablespoons balsamic vinegar
- Salt and pepper
- 1 medium yellow onion, cut into chunks
- 1 medium red pepper, cut into chunks
- 1 medium green pepper, cut into chunks

Instructions:

1 Mix the steak cubes with the balsamic vinegar, salt, and pepper before tossing them with olive oil.
2 Put the cubes, peppers, and onions on skewers, and then slide the cubes on. Oil the grate of a grill before preheating it to a high temperature.

3   Cook the kebabs on the grill for two to three minutes per side or until they reach the desired degree of doneness.

Nutrition Facts: 350 calories, 20g fat, 35g protein, 6.5g carbs

SEARED LAMB CHOPS WITH ASPARAGUS

Servings: 4
Prep Time: 5 minutes
Cook Time: 15 minutes

Ingredients:

- bone-in lamb chops
- Salt and pepper
- 1 tablespoon fresh chopped rosemary
- 1 tablespoon olive oil
- 1 tablespoon butter
- 16 spears of asparagus, cut into 2-inch chunks

Instructions:

1 Salt and pepper the lamb, then top with rosemary after seasoning with salt and pepper. Bring the oil to a boil in a large skillet over medium-high heat.
2 After adding the lamb chops, fry them for two to three minutes on each side in the hot pan. After removing the lamb chops to rest, bring the skillet with the butter back up to temperature.
3 After adding the asparagus, give the pan a quick turn to coat it, then cover it. Cook for four to six minutes, occasionally stirring, until soft but still crisp, then serve with the meat.

Nutrition Facts: 380 calories, 18.5g fat, 48g protein, 4.5g carbs

LEMON CHICKEN KEBABS WITH VEGGIES

Servings: 4
Prep Time: 10 minutes
Cook Time: 15 minutes

Ingredients:

- 1-pound boneless chicken thighs, cut into cubes
- ¼ cup olive oil
- tablespoons lemon juice
- 1 teaspoon minced garlic
- Salt and pepper
- 1 large yellow onion, cut into 2-inch chunks
- 1 large red pepper, cut into 2-inch chunks
- 1 large green pepper, cut into 2-inch chunks

Instructions:

1 Mix the chicken with the garlic, salt, and pepper before tossing it with olive oil, lemon juice, and garlic.

2   Put the chicken, onions, and peppers on skewers, and then slide the chicken onto the skewers. Prepare a grill for cooking over medium-high heat, then oil the grate surfaces.

3   When the chicken is ready, turn the skewers over and grill them for two to three minutes on each side.

Nutrition Facts: 360 calories, 21g fat, 34g protein, 8g carbs

Chapter 6 Desserts

COCONUT CHIA PUDDING

Servings: 6
Prep Time: 5 minutes
Cook Time: None

Ingredients:

- ¼ cups canned coconut milk
- 1 teaspoon vanilla extract
- Pinch salt
- ½ cup chia seeds

Instructions:

1   In a bowl, mix the vanilla extract, salt, and coconut milk together. To taste, sweeten with stevia after giving it a good stir. Stir in the chia seeds, then refrigerate the mixture overnight.
2   Place in bowls and garnish with chopped nuts or fruit before serving.

Nutrition Facts: 300 calories, 27.5g fat, 6g protein, 14.5g carbs

CHOCOLATE ALMOND BUTTER BROWNIES

Servings: 16
Prep Time: 15 minutes
Cook Time: 30 minutes

Ingredients:

- 1 cup almond flour
- ¾ cup unsweetened cocoa powder
- ½ cup shredded unsweetened coconut
- ½ teaspoon baking soda
- 1 cup coconut oil
- ½ cup canned coconut milk
- large eggs
- 1 ½ teaspoons liquid stevia extract
- ¼ cup almond butter

Instructions:

1   Prepare a square baking dish by lining it with foil and preheating the oven to 350 degrees Fahrenheit.

2   In a bowl, combine the almond flour, cocoa powder, coconut, and baking soda by whisking them together.
    In a separate bowl, combine the eggs, liquid stevia, coconut milk, and coconut oil by beating them together.

3   Mix the wet ingredients into the dry ones until almost all of the dry ingredients are wet, and then spread the mixture on the pan.
    In a microwave-safe bowl, melt the almond butter until it reaches a creamy consistency.

4   Drizzle the mixture over the chocolate batter, and then use a knife to gently swirl the two together.
    Allow cooling completely before cutting into 16 equal pieces after baking for 25 to 30 minutes or until the center has reached the desired consistency.

Nutrition Facts: 200 calories, 21g fat, 3g protein, 4.5g carbs

LEMON MERINGUE COOKIES

Servings: 8
Prep Time: 10 minutes
Cook Time: 60 minutes

Ingredients:

- large egg whites
- Pinch salt
- Liquid stevia extract, to taste
- 1 teaspoon lemon extract

Instructions:

1   Set the oven temperature to 225F. Line a baking sheet with parchment paper. In a bowl, whip the egg whites with a hand mixer until stiff peaks form.
2   After adding the salt and stevia, continue beating the mixture until it forms firm peaks. After incorporating the lemon extract, transfer the mixture to a piping bag.
3   Small rounds formed from the mixture should be piped onto the baking sheet. Bake for fifty to sixty minutes, until dry, then crack the door of the oven and let it cool for twenty minutes.

Nutrition Facts: 10 calories, 4g fat, 2g protein, 0g carbs

ALMOND FLOUR CUPCAKES

Servings: 12
Prep Time: 10 minutes
Cook Time: 25 minutes

Ingredients:

- ½ cups almond flour
- ¾ cup powdered erythritol
- 1 tablespoon baking powder
- ¼ teaspoon salt
- ¾ cup coconut oil, melted
- large eggs
- teaspoons vanilla extract

Instructions:

1   Set the oven to 350F. Line a muffin tin with paper cups. Almond flour, erythritol, baking powder, and salt should be mixed together in a bowl using a whisk.

2   In a separate bowl, combine the eggs, vanilla, and coconut oil by beating them together.

3   Combine the two separate ingredients and toss them together until they are thoroughly incorporated. Bake the dish for 22 to 25 minutes after placing the batter in the pan that has been prepared.

4   Wait five minutes before turning the cupcakes out onto a wire rack to finish cooling them in the pan.

Nutrition Facts: 260 calories, 26g fat, 6g protein, 5g carbs

COCONUT MACAROONS

Servings: 10
Prep Time: 10 minutes
Cook Time: 10 minutes

Ingredients:

- ½ cup unsweetened shredded coconut
- ¼ cup almond flour
- tablespoons powdered erythritol
- 1 tablespoon coconut oil
- 1 teaspoon vanilla extract
- ½ teaspoon coconut extract
- large egg whites

Instructions:

1   Turn the oven temperature up to 400F. Line a baking sheet with parchment paper.
2   In a bowl, mix the almond flour, shredded coconut, and erythritol. First, heat the coconut oil in a separate bowl, and then stir in the extracts using a whisk.

3   Combine the two different concoctions by giving them a good stir. The egg whites should be beaten in a bowl until they form stiff peaks before being folded into the batter.

4   Place heaping tablespoonfuls of the mixture on the prepared baking sheet. Bake the cookies for 7 to 9 minutes or until they have a light golden color around the edges.

Nutrition Facts: 105 calories, 9g fat, 2.5g protein, 3g carbs

VANILLA COCONUT MILK ICE CREAM

Servings: 6
Prep Time: 10 minutes
Cook Time: 30 minutes

Ingredients:

- 1 tablespoon coconut oil
- cups canned coconut milk, divided
- Liquid stevia extract, to taste
- 1 teaspoon vanilla extract

Instructions:

1 In a saucepan, melt the coconut oil, and then whisk in fifty percent of the can of
   coconut milk. Bring to a boil, then immediately reduce the heat and simmer for the
   next half an hour. Place in a bowl, sprinkle with stevia and wait until it reaches room
   temperature before serving.
2 After incorporating the vanilla essence, pour the leftover coconut milk into a bowl
   and set it aside. After whipping the coconut milk to the point where it forms stiff
   peaks, fold it into the other ingredients.
3 Place in a loaf pan and freeze until the mixture is solid.

Nutrition Facts: 205 calories, 21g fat, 2g protein, 4.5g carbs

PEPPERMINT DARK CHOCOLATE FUDGE

Servings: 16
Prep Time: 15 minutes
Cook Time: None

Ingredients:

- ½ cup coconut butter
- ⅓ cup coconut oil
- ounces dark chocolate chips
- 1 teaspoon peppermint extract
- Liquid stevia extract, to taste

Instructions:

1 Dark chocolate, coconut butter, and coconut oil should all be melted together in a double boiler over low heat.
2 Cook the mixture until all of the components have melted, then swirl it until it is smooth. Stir in the peppermint extract, then add stevia to taste for additional sweetness.

3   Spread the mixture in a baking dish that has been lined with parchment paper and chill it until it is hard. Take the fudge out of the dish and then cut it into squares so that it may be served.

Nutrition Facts: 165 calories, 15.5g fat, 1.5g protein, 8.5g carbs

LAYERED CHOCO-COCONUT BARS

Servings: 6
Prep Time: 20 minutes
Cook Time: None

Ingredients:

- 1 ½ cups shredded unsweetened coconut
- ½ cup canned coconut milk
- 1 teaspoon vanilla extract
- Liquid stevia extract to taste
- tablespoons coconut oil
- ¼ cup unsweetened cocoa powder

Instructions:

1   In a bowl, mix the shredded coconut, coconut milk, and vanilla extract together.
2   After giving it a thorough stir, sweeten it to taste with liquid stevia. Form a four-by-six-inch rectangle out of the coconut mixture and spread it out on a baking sheet lined with paper.

3   Before cutting into six bars and setting them aside, freeze for two hours or until the consistency of solid ice. The cocoa powder and stevia, to taste, should be whisked in after the coconut oil has been melted in the microwave.
4   After the chocolate mixture has cooled slightly, dip the bars in it until they are completely coated. Put the bars on a baking sheet, then place them in the refrigerator to make the chocolate more solid.

Nutrition Facts: 265 calories, 28g fat, 2g protein, 6g carbs

CINNAMON MUG CAKE

Servings: 1
Prep Time: 5 minutes
Cook Time: 1-minute

Ingredients:

- ⅓ cup almond flour
- 1 tablespoon powdered erythritol
- ½ teaspoon baking powder
- ¼ teaspoon ground cinnamon
- Pinch salt
- 1 large egg
- 1 tablespoon water
- 1 tablespoon coconut oil
- ½ teaspoon vanilla extract

Instructions:

1 Mix together the erythritol, baking powder, cinnamon, and salt in a bowl with the almond flour.

2   Whisk the egg, water, coconut oil, and vanilla extract together in a separate dish until combined. Stir the ingredients in the two bowls together, then pour them into a coffee mug that has been buttered.

3   Microwave on high for one minute. Serve.

Nutrition Facts: 395 calories, 36g fat, 13.5g protein, 8.5g carbs

RASPBERRY COCONUT MOUSSE

Servings: 6
Prep Time: 15 minutes
Cook Time: None

Ingredients:

- 1 ½ cups cashews, raw
- tablespoons lemon juice
- tablespoons water
- 1 ½ tablespoons coconut oil, melted
- 1 cup canned coconut milk (solids only)
- 1 teaspoon vanilla extract
- Liquid stevia extract, to taste
- ½ cup fresh raspberries, mashed slightly

Instructions:

1 Put the cashews, lemon juice, water, and coconut oil into a blender and process until the mixture is completely smooth.
2 After using a hand mixer to whip the coconut milk until it forms stiff peaks, beat in the vanilla extract and stevia until it tastes the way, you want it to.
3 After incorporating the whipped coconut milk into the cashew mixture, incorporate the berries into the cashew mixture.
4 Place in jars, then place in the refrigerator to chill for at least an hour.

Nutrition Facts: 325 calories, 29g fat, 6.5g protein, 15g carbs

CHOCOLATE COCONUT TRUFFLES

Servings: 12
Prep Time: 15 minutes
Cook Time: None

Ingredients:

- 1 cup coconut butter
- tablespoons unsweetened cocoa powder
- tablespoons unsweetened shredded coconut
- tablespoons instant coffee powder
- Liquid stevia extract, to taste
- tablespoons coconut oil, melted

Instructions:

1   In a microwave-safe bowl, melt the coconut butter and stir until it is completely smooth. Combine the cocoa powder, coffee powder, coconut, and stevia in a mixing bowl.
2   Coconut oil that has been melted should be used to grease the cups of an ice cube tray.

3 Put the chocolate-coconut mixture into the ice cube tray and press it firmly with a spoon.

4 Freeze for four hours, or until the substance is solid, then let it defrost at room temperature for fifteen minutes before serving.

Nutrition Facts: 290 calories, 28g fat, 3.5g protein, 11g carbs

CINNAMON-SPICED PUMPKIN BARS

Servings: 6
Prep Time: 15 minutes
Cook Time: None

Ingredients:

- ½ cup coconut oil
- ounces cream cheese, softened
- ¼ cup powdered erythritol
- 1 ½ teaspoons ground cinnamon
- ¼ cup pumpkin puree

Instructions:

1   Cream cheese and coconut oil should be combined in a saucepan and heated over medium-low heat. After the ingredients have melted and been mixed well, put them in a mixing bowl.
2   After mixing the erythritol and cinnamon together with a beater, spread the mixture on a parchment-lined plate. The pumpkin puree should be drizzled over the mixture, and then the mixture should be stirred with a knife.
3   Chill for at least four hours, and then cut it into bars to serve.

Nutrition Facts: 225 calories, 25g fat, 1.5g protein, 2g carbs

CHOCOLATE AVOCADO PUDDING

Servings: 4
Prep Time: 10 minutes
Cook Time: None

Ingredients:

- medium avocados, pitted and chopped
- ½ cup heavy cream
- tablespoons unsweetened cocoa powder
- to 3 tablespoons powdered erythritol
- 1 tablespoon almond flour
- 1 teaspoon vanilla extract

Instructions:

1 Put all of the ingredients into the food processor, and then give it a few pulses.
2 Blend on high until completely smooth, then transfer to individual serving cups. After it has thickened and become chilly, serve it.

Nutrition Facts: 275 calories, 26.5g fat, 3g protein, 11g carbs, 8g fiber, 3g net carbs

Conclusion

The ketogenic diet, also known as the "wonder diet," is still the gold standard for those who wish to reduce their body fat percentage and prevent the onset of any diseases. Eighty years ago, people began exploring the benefits of a diet that prioritized fat and protein above carbohydrates. This diet eventually became known as the "ketogenic diet." With its novel strategy, it encourages the body to use stored fat for fuel instead of glucose. As little as two weeks on a ketogenic diet can transform your body into a fat-burning machine. Easy weight loss, reduced cardiovascular risk, and protection against stroke and certain cancers are just a few of the many health benefits you'll enjoy while following this diet. Many people's health depends on the fact that the ketogenic diet can effectively halt or even reverse the onset of diabetes. This comprehensive ketogenic diet guide is all you need if you're seeking a diet that will leave you feeling more pleased and energized while also healing your body from the harm caused by years of eating a high-carbohydrate, high-sugar diet.

Printed in Great Britain
by Amazon

40779966R00071